P9-CNB-885

No Borders

Kigliqangittuq

By DARLA EVYAGOTAILAK
and MINDY WILLETT

Photographs by
Tessa Macintosh

LIBRARY
FRANKLIN PIERCE UNIVERSITY
RINDGE, NH 03461

Fifth House Ltd.
A Fitzhenry & Whiteside Company
195 Allstate Parkway
Markham, Ontario L3R 4T8
1-800-387-9776
www.fifthhousepublishers.ca

THE CANADA COUNCIL | LE CONSEIL DES ARTS
FOR THE ARTS | DU CANADA
SINCE 1957 | DEPUIS 1957

ONTARIO ARTS COUNCIL
CONSEIL DES ARTS DE L'ONTARIO

MIX
Paper from
responsible sources
FSC   FSC® C016245
www.fsc.org

First published in the
United States in 2013 by
Fitzhenry & Whiteside
311 Washington Street
Brighton, Massachusetts
02135

CURR
E
99
.E7
E99
2013

Copyright © 2013 Mindy Willett and Darla Evyagotailak

All rights reserved. No part of this publication may be reproduced, stored in a retrieval system, or transmitted, in any form or by any means, electronic, mechanical, recording, or otherwise, without the prior written permission of the publisher, except in the case of a reviewer, who may quote brief passages in a review to print in a magazine or newspaper, or broadcast on radio or television. In the case of photocopying or other reprographic copying, users must obtain a license from Access Copyright.

Cover and interior design by John Luckhurst
Map design by Dot van Vliet
Photography by Tessa Macintosh
Additional photographs by: Mindy Willett (Kate and Darla high-five, page 2; Kate and Roy kissing baby, page 6; Darla square dancing, page 9; Roy sharing quaq, page 12; Kate chopping ice, page 14; camp scene, page 18; Darla and Mary embrace, page 23; three generations of Joes, page 26; Darla in sled box, page 30; Tessa, page 34); Ernest Mayer, Winnipeg Art Gallery (Helen Kalvak, Canadian [Ulukhaktok], c. 1901-1984, Printmaker: Harry Egotak, 1925-?, Two People Dancing, c. 1970, stonecut on paper [45.9 x 61.3 cm], page 4); Damian Panayi (Doreen and Doneen, page 7); Donna Stephania (Charles Amos, page 27); Richard S. Finnie, Library and Archives Canada, PA-101172 (Copper Inuit dance in a snowhouse, Coronation Gulf NWT, 1931, page 39); Government of the Northwest Territories Department of Education, Culture and Employment (NWT maps, page 39).

Series editorial by Meaghan Craven
Proofread by Kirsten Craven

The type in this book is set in 10-on-15-point Trebuchet Regular and 10-on-13-point Tekton Oblique.

Fifth House acknowledges with thanks the Canada Council for the Arts and the Ontario Arts Council for their support of our publishing program. We acknowledge the financial support of the Government of Canada through the Book Publishing Industry Development Program (BPIDP) for our publishing activities.

The authors would like to thank Canadian North, The Nunavut Department of Education, BHP Billiton, the Canadian Ranger Program, the Kitikmeot Inuit Association, and the Prince of Wales Northern Heritage Centre for financial and in-kind assistance leading to the completion of this book.

Printed by Friesens Corporation in Altona, MB, Canada, in January 2013. Job #80564.

2013 / 1

Library and Archives Canada Cataloguing in Publication

Evyagotailak, Darla
No borders = Kigliqangittuq / by Darla Evyagotailak and Mindy Willett; photographs by Tessa Macintosh.

(The land is our storybook)
Text in English with some words in Inuinnaqtun.
ISBN 978-1-927083-07-9

1. Evyagotailak, Darla—Juvenile literature.
2. Evyagotailak, Darla—Family—Juvenile literature.
3. Inuit—Nunavut—Kugluktuk—Biography—Juvenile literature. 4. Inuit—Northwest Territories—Ulukhaktok—Biography—Juvenile literature. 5. Inuit—Nunavut—Kugluktuk—Social life and customs—Juvenile literature.
6. Inuit—Northwest Territories—Ulukhaktok—Social life and customs—Juvenile literature. 7. Kugluktuk (Nunavut)—Biography—Juvenile literature. 8. Ulukhaktok (N.W.T.)—Biography—Juvenile literature. I. Willett, Mindy, 1968-II. Title. III. Title: Kigliqangittuq. IV. Series: Land is our storybook.

E99.E7E99 2012   j971.9'550049710092   C2012-905437-2

Acknowledgements

The making of this book was a wonderful journey. We have tried to share life in two communities across a border through two territories. We could not have managed this without the help of so many people.

In particular we would like to thank Darla's mother, Susie Evyagotailak, and great-grandparents, Kate and Roy Inuktalik, and Randy Allen. Thank you for taking us on the trip of a lifetime. Sadly, only 10 months after leading this journey, Roy passed away. His skills in so many areas and the loving way in which he shared with others are deeply missed.

From Kugluktuk we want to thank: Joe Evyagotailak for explaining the history of the border between Nunavut and the NWT and what it means to have a strong foundation (*tunngavik*); Darla's mom, Doreen, and the entire family; Darla's soccer team, including Coach Jessica Van Overbeek, Carla Algona, Beverly Anablak, Aislyn Bolt, Iris Bolt, Jenny Klengenberg, Tundra Kuliktana, Emerald MacDonald, and Keisha Westwood; the amazing fiddlers and dancers at the community square-dance competition. Thank you, Kugluktuk Drummers and Dancers for posing for pictures in -40°C. For the joy you bring when you dance and sing, *quana* to Theresa Adamache, Andrew Atatahak, Colleen Nivingalok, Margo Nivingalok, Priscilla Niptanatiak, Calla Pedersen, and Myles and Calvin Pedersen.

The generosity of the people of Ulukhaktok was much appreciated. In particular, we would like to thank: Emily Kudlak, Koral Kudlak, Mona Kudlak, and Rene Taipana. Canadian Rangers Adam Kudlak, Roland Notaina, and Rob Stevens helped us with logistics, gas, and shared knowledge.

For her thoughtful and patient editing we would like to thank Meaghan Craven, and for help with translations, editing, and design we thank Jamie Bastedo, Millie Kuliktana, Donna Stephania, and Dot van Vliet. Thank you, John Luckhurst, for all the skill and ideas you brought to designing this book.

Tessa would like to thank to her friend and husband, Mike Freeland, for recounting his many adventures, amongst them, hunting with Inuit on Holman Island back in the old days.

Mindy would like to note that she moved to Coppermine, NWT (now Kugluktuk, Nunavut), in 1996 with a new teaching certificate in hand. Like many teachers before her, she learned more from the students than they from her, and she will be forever grateful to each one of them. The community opened their doors, shared traditions, food, cups of tea, tears, and much laughter. There is much non-Aboriginal Canadians should know about how colonialism affected and continues to impact on Aboriginal peoples in Canada. In her small way, Mindy hopes that this book can help others learn about the incredible, strong, dignified people of the North. *Piqpaguhugluta kihiani.*

Left: Look at the trim on the parkas Darla and her family members are wearing. The trim featured at the top of most pages in the book is from the parka Darla's mother is wearing (second from left).

To Uncle Tolok. I miss you a lot and wish you were here.

Grandpapa Roy Inuktalik, I dedicate this book to you.

Love,
Ukaliannuaq

No Borders

Kigliqangittuq

By **DARLA EVYAGOTAILAK**
and **MINDY WILLETT**

Photographs by
Tessa Macintosh

FIFTH
HOUSE

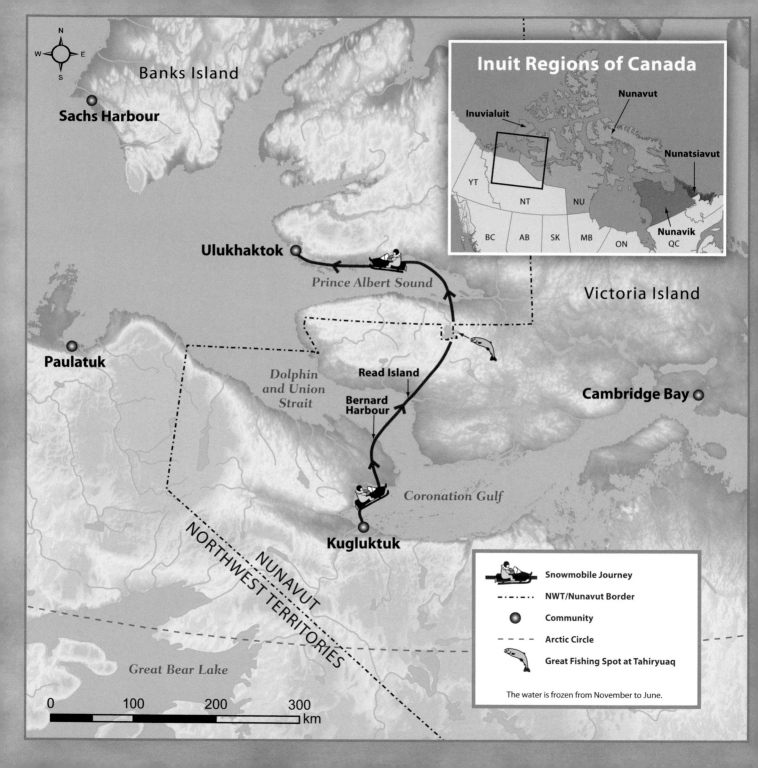

Banks Island

Sachs Harbour

Ulukhaktok

Prince Albert Sound

Victoria Island

Paulatuk

Dolphin and Union Strait

Read Island

Bernard Harbour

Cambridge Bay

Coronation Gulf

Kugluktuk

NUNAVUT

NORTHWEST TERRITORIES

Great Bear Lake

Inuit Regions of Canada

Inuvialuit

Nunavut

Nunatsiavut

YT

NT

NU

BC | AB | SK | MB | ON

Nunavik

QC

Snowmobile Journey

NWT/Nunavut Border

Community

Arctic Circle

Great Fishing Spot at Tahiryuaq

The water is frozen from November to June.

0   100   200   300
km

Kinauvilli?

Kinauvilli means "Who are you?" My answer to that question is, *Darlauyunga. Angayuqqaatka Qihuulik Evyagotailarlu. Kugluktumiutauyunga.* This means, "I am Darla and my parents are Joe and Susie Evyagotailak, and I am from Kugluktuk."

My mother told me that asking *kinauvilli* is a good, traditional way to greet a stranger because it helps others understand who you are, who your family is, and where you come from. It is important to discover connections between you and others: how you might be related or how your grandfather might have hunted with theirs. If two people are connected, they're more likely to help one another.

I live in Kugluktuk, Nunavut, but much of my family lives in Ulukhaktok, NWT. Both are small towns. Although on opposite sides of a territorial border, there is no real border for us as many of us are related. Our language is called Inuinnaqtun. I can sometimes understand what people are saying, but I can't speak my language. That makes me sad, and sometimes I feel like an outsider. I don't want to feel like that. I want to know more about who I am and where I come from.

In this book you'll follow me on a journey from Kugluktuk to Ulukhaktok. I want to share what my life is like, both the good and the hard. *Quana* means "thank you" in my language. *Quana* for listening.

Darla

Darla Evyagotailak

Strong Women

Helen→Rene→Kate→Susie→Doreen→Darla

I know I come from a long line of strong women. My birth mother is Doreen. I call her Mom, but I was adopted by Mom's parents, Joe and Susie, who I call Mother and Dad. They also raised two boys, Charles Amos and Joe Junior, and three other girls, including Mom and my sisters, Tracy and Shelley.

Darla calls her great-grandmother, Kate, Grandma-ma. They have a lot of fun together, especially when they are cruising on the snow machine. Here, 74-year-old Grandma-ma drives up alongside Darla to give her a high five.

Darla sews with her nanak or great-great-grandma, Rene Taipana, who is Kate's mom. Rene lives in Ulukhaktok, and while she is surely over 90 years, no one knows exactly how old she is.

Although we don't live in the same house, my birthmom is still a big part of my life. Sometimes when I'm not getting along with Mother and Dad, I go and see her. Being a teenager isn't always easy, and when I'm moody it's good to have another place to go.

After many years watching her mother, Susie, dice caribou meat with an ulu, Darla can do it, too.

From left to right: Darla's mother Susie (biologically her grandmother), her great-grandmother Kate, Darla, and her birth mom Doreen. They are softening a caribou hide from Darla's first caribou harvest.

Darla (right) learned the dance steps to the song Whale Tail from her mom, Doreen. The dance celebrates the joy of cutting off the tips of the whale tail, which are delicious to eat. This is a Western Arctic dance.

I also spend a lot of time with Grandma-ma Kate. She is a very special person to me. One day, I dressed up in my fancy parka for our Spirit Days at school, and she came to my house and drew the tattoos of her grandmother, Helen Kalvak, on my face. When I look at pictures of her, I think she is so beautiful. I don't know why we stopped tattooing. Someday, I'm going to get the very same tattoos.

There are six generations between these two strong women, Helen and Darla.

Helen Kalvak

Helen Kalvak was born in an iglu at Tahiryuaq (see map) and lived a traditional life off the land. She was an incredible artist. Helen's art often reveals her understanding of the world of an angatkuq (shaman) and of singing and drum-dancing. One of her prints, Two People Dancing (c. 1970), shows how the people's caribou and seal parkas were decorated with white fur from a rabbit and wolverine with weasel tassels. Hats were made of loon and weasel for this dance called Apkuangmiut, *or Loon Dance.*

I feel connected to the lives of my ancestors through the stories Grandma-ma tells. She was born in an iglu, and I was born in a hospital. I can't imagine what her life was like when she was my age. She is a good sewer and dancer. I'm trying to learn to be a good dancer, too. One of our hardest dances is called the Loon Dance, *Apkuangmiut*. You have to move your body, like you do when hula hooping, to try to get the weasel tassel, attached to the loon beak at the top of the hat, to swing all around the loon beak without getting tangled.

Kate sewed this loon hat for the youth dancers.

The Loon Dance is performed to welcome the sun after a long winter, or to welcome people when they visit from other camps. Colleen Nivingalok, who is in the Kugluktuk dance group with Darla, dances Apkuangmiut with all her heart. She learned these dances from the Elders, and her goal is to pass them on to younger dancers like Darla.

My full name is Darla Rose Hikalgok Evyagotailak. Hikalgok is my name in my language, Inuinnaqtun. We believe that a person's spirit never dies. When a child is named after someone who has passed away, that child carries the spirit, the personality, and the talents of the person she or he was named after. Hikalgok used to take care of my dad, Joe, when he was young. They say when I was young and my dad was sleeping, I would always stay up and watch him. I truly am Hikalgok.

Our Words

attiaqhi —	the one who named you
attiaq —	the one you named or are related to through your name
atiq —	someone you are named after
atiruarut —	someone you share a nickname with
haunittiak —	someone you share a name with
tiguaq —	adopted child

As is common, Darla was adopted by her grandparents. When you are adopted, you are called a tiguaq. Here, Darla and her dad, Joe, share a meal of frozen Arctic char.

Because baby Marion is named after one of their best friends, Darla's great-grandparents, Kate and Roy, have a special bond with her. They talk to her as if she is their friend. Here Roy is saying to his friend, "What, you have nothing to say to me now?"

Darla's sister, Shelley, is also a tiguaq. Her Inuinnaqtun name is Keadjuk. She and Darla carry the names of a married couple. Darla calls Shelley, "my little husband."

6

Darla's little sister, Doneen, was originally named after her late grandpa. As a baby, she was ill. Doreen believed her baby couldn't tolerate her name. Doreen was told Doneen's grandpa didn't want too many people named after him. An Elder advised Doreen to change the baby's name. As soon as she had a new name, she got better.

Darla's dad was named Evyagotailak at birth. In those days, Inuit did not have last names. But the Canadian government insisted that Inuit take last names, and many, like Joe, used their given names as last names. The Elders still call him Evyagotailak.

Kinauvilli?

Aivgak was a very good drum-dancer. Calvin, who is named after him, is a good drum-dancer, too.

I am 16 years old and in grade 10. My town, Kugluktuk, is the westernmost community in Nunavut. Some kids say Kugluktuk is boring. Sometimes I agree, but it can be a fun place to live, too, and besides, my parents always tell me, "You have to make your own fun."

The background image shows the view from town.

Darla is in the pre-trades program at her high school, hoping to be a carpenter someday. She and her classmate, Marcelle Miyok, work on a model of a house in her favourite class, drafting.

Left: Between classes, Darla chats with her friend, Jenny, about the square-dance competition.

Practically the entire town shows up to participate in and watch the Square-dance Showdown. Darla's youth group takes the grand prize.

Left: Darla (back row centre) plays defence for the Grizzlies, Kugluktuk High School's indoor soccer team. Because of the long winters, soccer is an indoor sport.

Long ago, to stay fit during winters spent mostly inside the iglu, Inuit invented sports that allowed them to keep up their strength within a small space. Now, these Arctic sports are practiced for fun and competitions. Here, Andrew, a drum-dancer, shows off the two-foot high kick.

Aullaaqtugut (Travelling)

It can be fun in town, but I need to go out on the land to find out where my family comes from. Because my great-grandparents miss their family and the land where they were born, they often travel between Kugluktuk and Ulukhaktok. This year, Mother and I went with them. From Kugluktuk, we travelled by land and sea ice to a great ice-fishing spot and then on to Ulukhaktok, where Mother was born. Before we left, I was nervous because I knew I'd be cold and it would be hard, but I was also excited.

Kate picks up some groceries. During the trip, they will eat caribou and fish, but Darla is used to eating "town food."

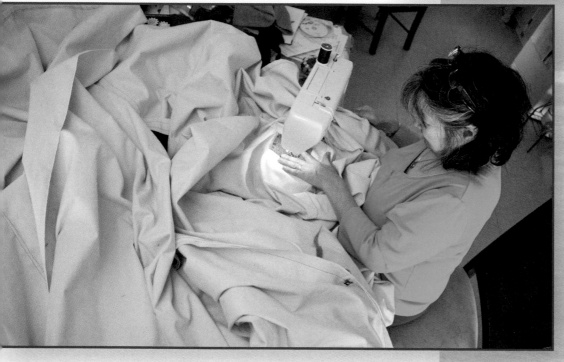

Susie sews a new canvas tent (tupiq) for the journey. The tent will be small so they won't have to use too much fuel to heat it.

Joe helps pack up the sled box. To travel the 600 km to Ulukhaktok, it takes about 5 days, depending on weather and ice conditions.

When we were ready to leave Kugluktuk, Dad came down to the sea ice to say goodbye. He couldn't come with us because he had to work, but he did help us pack for the 5-day trip. We had to be prepared to be out on the land for longer than 5 days, though, just in case something happened. There are no stores or places to get help out there, so we needed to be able to depend on ourselves.

Our travelling group included Mother, my great-grandparents, me, and Randy, who lives next door to my great-grandparents. They have taught him a lot, and he came along so he could learn and so we would have an extra pair of strong hands.

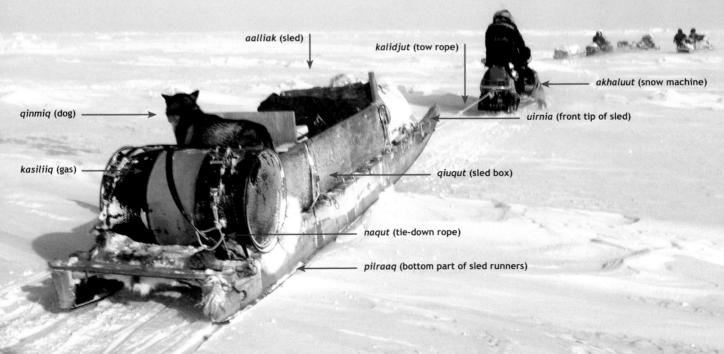

aalliak (sled)

kalidjut (tow rope)

akhaluut (snow machine)

qinmiq (dog)

uirnia (front tip of sled)

kasiliiq (gas)

qiuqut (sled box)

naqut (tie-down rope)

pilraaq (bottom part of sled runners)

Before we left, Grandpa-pa did one last check of everyone's sled box to make sure everything was tied down properly and that we were all comfortable and safe. He then got on his snow machine and headed out. The rest of us followed. On the first day we travelled to Bernard Harbour. It normally takes about 4 hours, but it took longer as Grandpa-pa slowed down for his passenger on the sled (me). You can see the route we took on the map at the front of the book.

Roy shaves off pieces of quaq for the group.

During a break, the travellers eat bannock, frozen raw fish, or caribou (any frozen raw meat is called quaq), and drink hot chocolate and tea. Kate always fed Randy first. His youth and strength were important to the entire group's survival.

Even though I was warm in my sleeping bag, I pulled myself out of bed and into the cold morning. When Grandpa-pa started getting ready to leave again, we all followed him without him needing to tell us what to do. Dad always taught me that if people are being lazy, they pull all the others down with them. If everyone works together, it's not so bad.

Above: Even though the temperature is -40° C and the wind is gusting, Darla fills some pots with snow, which will later be melted down for tea.

Right: It is important to bring enough gas: there are no gas stations along the way!

Grandpa-pa is tough. He is 74 years old, and he led our trip. He packed up our sleds, helped us with our tents, and taught us many things, like the importance of putting everything back into the sled box at night, so we don't lose our stuff in a snow storm.

Susie pounds the snow off clothes and bedding before putting them away or in the tent. If she doesn't do this, the snow will melt. Wearing wet clothes when out on the land raises the risk of developing hypothermia.

At the age of 74, Kate can drive her own snow machine all day long, set up camp, prepare a meal, chop the ice, and still have time to teach everyone about Inuit traditions.

Travelling over the sea ice can be rough. The leader has to navigate the ice to find a safe route. Some-times, when the sleds get stuck, everyone has to help.

14

Navigating the Land

Roy uses his life experience when he travels on the land. He knows that the prevailing wind usually blows the snow in the same direction. As he is driving, he can feel the shape of the drifts under his sled runners. He also recognizes different landmarks and can navigate, even in a storm. He jokes that he doesn't need a GPS because he has an internal "EPS" ("Eskimo" Positioning System).

Darla doesn't have Roy's experience on the land, but through the Junior Ranger program she is learning how to use a GPS.

O ur land is so peaceful and beautiful, but it is also big and scary. If I were alone out there, I couldn't survive. But Grandpa-pa, when he looks out on the same area, he just sees his home. He tries to help me understand how he knows where we're going, and that makes the land less scary for me. I'm still glad I'm not alone out here, though.

It took us 3 days to make it to Tahiryuaq: the fishing spot, which is right on the border. The land we travelled over had big hills and the ice was rough. The wind blew and it was very cold, but I was cozy because I wore Mother's *hikhik* (ground squirrel) parka.

Our Stories

Tunngavik (A Strong Foundation)

Told by Joe Evyagotailak

The border between the NWT and Nunavut is mostly straight except for a little notch so the communities of Kugluktuk and Ulukhaktok can share one of the best trout-fishing lakes around. Not too long ago, at this lake, people from around Ulukhaktok would meet the people from the mainland. They got together to trade driftwood for copper and to socialize, hold dances, and fish. We call the lake Quunnguq, which means "a place with a narrow spot," but it is also referred to as Tahiryuaq, or Big Lake.

Nunavut means "Our Land." Inuit have always known this is our land, our home, but the Canadian government also thought it was their land. In the 1970s, a group of young Inuit leaders worked very hard to help get our land back through a land claim. In 1999 it became official, and what had been the NWT became two territories. Coming up with a border between the NWT and Nunavut was one of the hardest decisions we had to make. We had to give up a lot of land, and many of our relatives live on the other side of the border in communities like Ulukhaktok. But, just like the caribou, who don't see the border, we continue to travel, hunt, and fish on our shared lands as we have for thousands of years.

Over 10 years have passed since Nunavut was created and we Inuit still have many struggles ahead to regain our independence, identity, and pride. We must give our kids a strong foundation, or tunngavik, so they will know who they are and where they come from.

Joe explains to Darla how the border between the NWT and Nunavut was negotiated.

17

Setting Up Camp

When we got to the lake, Grandpa-pa did a little dance. He was happy and said he could almost taste the fish we were going to catch. First, though, we had to make camp.

1. Find a good flat spot for your tent, then lay the tent down. Pound the stakes into the ground. Put the wooden poles inside the tent to make it stand up.

2. Pack snow around the outside of the tent to hold it down and provide extra insulation from the cold.

3. Make the inside of the tent cozy. First, remove snow from the foot of the "bed." Make sure you leave snow in a space in the corner for a table.

4. Set up the bed. The first layer is caribou skin, fur down. This helps keep the mattresses dry.

5. When the tent is a warm and comfortable home, hook up the two-way radio so you can call home and let everyone know where you are spending the night.

After our camp was set up we could get down to the business of fishing. I'm not very patient. When we were fishing, I got tired of jigging, so I passed Grandma-ma my jigger and, after two seconds she got a fish. Too bad I didn't wait!

Darla uses an ice scoop, or illaut, to clear the hole of ice.

Randy and Roy chisel through the thick ice to reach the water. Then, they put snow blocks around the hole to block the wind. Roy makes a seat out of snow and covers it with caribou hides.

Roy sharpens the ice chisel known in Inuinnaqtun as a tuuq.

20

Kate and Darla jig for trout. Jigging is the term for ice fishing with a hook and bait on the end of a stick.

Susie scoops some water out of the ice-fishing hole to fill the soup pot.

The family gathers in Kate and Roy's tent to share a meal made from the fish they caught.

Randy holds up one of the many ihuuq (lake trout) they caught. They stopped fishing only when the sled boxes were full.

After two days of ice fishing, we had filled the sled boxes with lake trout. We headed on to Ulukhaktok. It was a long day of travelling—over 12 hours of being bounced around in a box, riding on top of 50 frozen fish!

When we arrived, it was late at night, and we felt cold and hungry. But it was all worth it because my entire family was waiting for us. I was so happy that my *nanak*, Rene, was still awake, wanting to welcome us. We all piled into Auntie Ida's house, where she fed us a big pot of caribou soup.

To celebrate the arrival of the visitors from Kugluktuk, the community hosted a traditional feast, with dancing and drumming.

Kate's sister, Mary, welcomes Darla home to Ulukhaktok.

Above: Darla and Great-great-grandma Rene (whom she calls Nanak) share a kunik (kiss). Rene got a ride down to the sea ice on a snow machine to meet them.

Kate's mom, Rene (left), Roy, and Kate are so happy to have a chance to visit with all their family.

23

Being in Ulukhaktok was a lot of fun. I got to hang out with all my cousins and cruise around on the snow machine. Mother insisted that I visit my Elders. She said they won't be around much longer, and I should learn from them while I have the chance. It's fun to hang out with my friends, but I did what Mother said and visited with Nanak. Even though it was difficult because I cannot speak Inuinnaqtun and she can't speak English, we did a lot of talking with our eyes. I spent the most special moments in Ulukhaktok with her.

Darla and her cousins look out over Ulukhaktok, which means "the place where ulu parts are found." An ulu is a moon-shaped knife. The houses are spread out along the oceanfront, with the school and store behind.

The Land is our Storybook
Reading and Writing the Land

The people from Ulukhaktok, are known as the long-distance walkers. Not long ago they spent the winters on the sea ice, and in the spring followed the trail to the stone tent rings that showed where to camp and collect eggs. In the summer they would continue their long walk inland to the caribou calving grounds. In the fall they prepared caribou hides for their winter clothing and started the long walk back to the sea ice. To help the young people understand what life was like in traditional times, the Elders quilted their story. The quilt, called The Long-distance Walkers, *shows how the people "write" on the land by leaving messages, such as the stone markers for caches of food, and how they "read" these markers on the land (as well as the sky, stars, and weather) to know how and where to travel.*

Darla's cousin, Emily, describes the trails followed by their ancestors.

Three generations of Joes: (left to right) Joe Junior, Charles Joe, and Joe Senior. Charles Joe gets his name from his uncle, Charles Amos, who died.

When I'm with my grandparents I learn a lot about the old ways, how hard it was and yet how happy people were. They lived through times when they had nothing to eat. Nowadays, we have enough to eat, but they say we gave up a lot to have the "easy life." I don't know what they mean. It doesn't feel easy to me. I think life can be really hard right now. Sometimes there is a lot of sadness around me, and I wonder why. It's really hard to talk about, and I don't always have the words to describe how I feel.

Charles Amos

The oldest son in Darla's family, Charles Amos, was one of the first graduates of the new high school in Kugluktuk. He was bright and handsome. Everyone loved him. Like too many others, he took his own life in March 1997. The North has Canada's highest rate of suicide. No one knows exactly why. Hopefully, by talking about these tragedies, fewer of them will happen.

Charles Amos holding his baby son.

This sadness can make people do things that shatter families. I don't really remember my older brother, Charles Amos, but I still think about him and what he did. When I was a baby he committed suicide. I don't know why, but I do know he left a hole in our family.

Becoming Strong

Even though things can be hard, Grandma-ma always says, "Don't worry, be happy!" She reminds me that things will get better. Many adults try to help us young people to be strong and not give in to sadness. It's sure hard, though, because sometimes we don't even understand what they are saying.

Roy shows Darla how to feel through the layers of the snow with an unaaq (snow probe). For an iglu to be strong, the snow has to be consistent throughout an entire block. The best snow to use has been blown by the wind. When you walk on top of the snow it should be strong.

Roy is an expert iglu builder and explains to Darla how to add the last block. Inuit don't live in iglus anymore, but Elders know it's important for youth to learn how to build them. If you are out on the land and get lost, an iglu can save your life.

Still, Elders are working hard to help us learn about our traditions and keep our language. Having the words to say how you feel is really important!

For a long time, the tradition of drumming and dancing, or qilaudjaqtut, was banned by the Canadian government. Today, the youth (Darla is centre back row) are strong, proud, talented dancers, just like their ancestors, photographed here in a snowhouse in Kugluktuk in 1931.

After a week visiting family in Ulukhaktok, it was time to go back home. As we travelled back to Kugluktuk, I sat in the sled box and looked out across our beautiful land. It doesn't matter what side of the border we live on: we're all the same. This is where my ancestors not only survived but thrived. Their strength and ability is the reason I am here, and that makes me proud.

During a break on the way back to Kugluktuk, Darla plays with her dog, Kuni.

I am thankful that my grandparents want to teach me about my culture and traditions. It makes me feel good inside. I know I have a lot to learn, but with a little hard work and the love of my family, I'll make it.
I am strong.

Quana.

All the Details!

Pronouncing Our Words

Kugluktuk — *Qur-look-took* —
the community where Darla lives

Ulukhaktok — *Oo-look-hak-tok* —
the community where Darla's mother was born

Inuinnaqtun — *In-nooo-in-nak-toon* —
the language spoken in Ulukhaktok, Kugluktuk, and Cambridge Bay

Kinauvitli — *Keen-owe-veet-ly* —
a greeting: Who are you?

Quana — *Kwan-a* —
thank you

What's in a Name?

What's in a name? Lots! When Darla was born, her town was called Coppermine, Northwest Territories. Neither of these place names belonged to the Inuit people.

Today, her town is called Kugluktuk, Nunavut. Many place names in the North are returning to traditional names that are born of the language of the community.

Place Name Then	Place Name Now
Holman, NWT, was named for J.R. Holman, a member of the 1853 expedition searching for Arctic explorer John Franklin.	Ulukhaktok means "the place where ulu parts are found." It was officially renamed in 2006.
Frobisher Bay was named for Martin Frobisher, who, during his search for the Northwest Passage in 1576, became the first European to visit the bay.	Iqaluit is the capital of Nunavut. It means "the place of fish." *Iqaluk* means "one fish" and *uit* makes the word plural.
The name "Coppermine" was first used by Europeans who visited the area and saw Inuit using copper tools. They hoped to find enough copper to build a mine. They never did, but "Coppermine" was put on maps and it stuck for 100 years.	Kugluktuk refers to the fast-flowing waters up the river from town. The community's name was officially changed from Coppermine to Kugluktuk in 1996.
Not so long ago the Northwest Territories covered almost all of Canada. The last division was in 1999 when the Northwest Territories divided into two.	The eastern territory became Nunavut, which means "our land" in Inuktitut.

Inuit Identity Tags

Starting in the early 1940s, the Canadian government wanted to keep track of how many Inuit there were. Government officials found Inuit names hard to pronounce and spell, so all Inuit were given a number on a small brown disc on a string. The only way Inuit could identify themselves to the government was by means of these tags. People living east of Gjoa Haven received "E" numbers and people living to the west received "W" numbers.

Susie's number was W2-814.

The Word "Eskimo"

Roy used the term "Eskimo" when he jokingly talked about his "EPS" or "Eskimo Positioning System." For a long time, Inuit were referred to as "Eskimos," and in Alaska the term is still used. The root of the word is not fully agreed upon, but one thing for certain is it is not the term Inuit use for themselves. *Inuk* is singular (one person). The *-uit* at the end of *Inuit* makes it plural. So, Inuit means "the people."

Tattoos in Inuit Culture

Traditionally many Inuit women had tattoos, which were considered beautiful. When Christian missionaries came north, they made the Inuit feel that many of their traditions—tattooing included—were wrong. As a result, tattooing and other traditions were almost wiped out. Today, some Inuit women are reclaiming the art of facial tattooing.

Susie shows her daughters her W-tag.

The Evolution of the NWT Boundary

Before 1870, North-West Territories was the name for the land north and west of central Canada. Over the years, new provinces were carved out of the territory and older provinces expanded their boundaries. Compare these two maps with the one at the front of the book. A lot has changed in the North!

About the Authors and Photographer

Darla Evyagotailak is a 16-year-old girl from Kugluktuk, Nunavut. She loves to play soccer, square dance, and drive around with her friends on her snow machine or quad. She goes out on the land to learn more about her culture. Darla wants to be a carpenter someday, but she's remaining open to other options. *No Borders* is her first book.

Mindy Willett is an educator currently living in Yellowknife. *No Borders* is the 8th book she has co-written in the series, *The Land is Our Storybook*. This book is particularly near and dear to her heart as she worked as a teacher in Kugluktuk and met Darla on her very first day in town when Darla was a new baby. Mindy feels indebted to the many Kugluktumiut who have made her feel loved, welcome, and a part of the community.

Tessa Macintosh a long-time northern photographer, has worked with the *Native Press* newspaper and the NWT government. Based in Yellowknife, she now runs a sweet little bed and breakfast and enjoys a career as a freelance photographer. The first time Tessa was in Ulukhaktok (then Holman) was over 30 years ago: this time the assignment was a little more challenging! She was grateful to be in the expert care of Kate and Roy during the long, bumpy, 600-km sled trip during which the travellers experienced a -40°C wind chill.

The Land is Our Storybook

Titles in *The Land is Our Storybook* series, all co-written by Mindy Willett and illustrated by Tessa Macintosh:

We Feel Good Out Here,
  by Julie-Ann André

The Delta is My Home,
  by Tom McLeod

Living Stories,
  by Therese Zoe and
  Philip Zoe

Come and Learn with Me,
  by Sheyenne Jumbo

Proud to be Inuvialuit,
  by James Pokiak

The Caribou Feed Our Soul,
  by Pete Enzoe

At the Heart of It,
  by Raymond Taniton

No Borders,
  by Darla Evyagotailak

The first six titles in the series are also available in French!

Franklin Pierce University

00201214

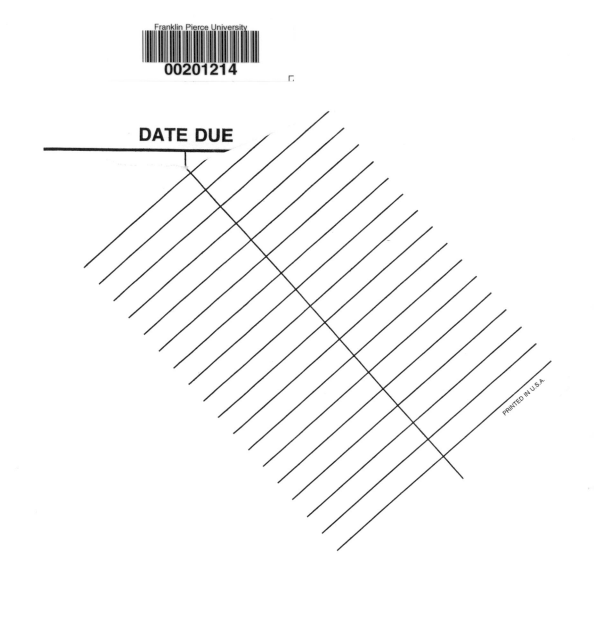

DATE DUE

PRINTED IN U.S.A.